HEAR OUR VOICE, HEAR OUR STORY

By
Emiliana Guereca
Deena Katz
Hanieh Jodat

Copyright © 2017 Women's March LA Foundation. All rights reserved throughout the world. No part of this book may be reproduced in any form except in the case of brief quotations embodied in articles or reviews without the express written permission from the authors or Putnam & Smith Publishing Company. Women's March Los Angeles is registered trademark of Women's March LA Foundation and Putnam & Smith Publishing Company, Encino, California.

Women's March Los Angeles: Hear Our Voice, Hear Our Story
by
Emiliana Guereca
Deena Katz
Hanieh Jodat

Copyright © 2017
Putnam & Smith Publishing Company
Women's March Los Angeles Foundation

Cover & Book Design by: Connie Jacobs
Cover Concept: Morgan Geffner

Distributed by:
Putnam & Smith Publishing Company
15915 Ventura Boulevard, Suite 101
Encino, California 91436
www.putnamandsmithpublishing.com

Library of Congress Control Number: 2017946611

ISBN: 978-1-939986-18-4

Printed in the United States of America

FOREWORD

On January 21, 2017, hundreds of thousands of women in Los Angeles County linked arms to send a message to our nation's leaders. That message still rings true: "We are here, we are strong, and together, we will continue to fight for equality."

As I walked the streets of Downtown LA that morning, I felt the pride, strength, and determination propel us forward. Women in all shapes, sizes and skin tones banded together, speaking in a singular, powerful, beautiful voice, "We will not be ignored or silenced – we will be heard."

Opinions have always had the power to divide, but on that January day, the clamor for a more equitable society was louder than any difference of opinion. We heard one voice demanding equality for all, regardless of one's race, ethnicity, national origin, citizenship status, socioeconomic status, age, disability, religion, sex, gender identity or expression.

As a daughter of immigrants, a sister, and an elected official who has had the honor of representing millions of men and women, I was reminded of the power of unity, the strength behind a common cause, and our duty to ourselves, vulnerable members of society, and future generations to speak up and demand justice for all. This includes immigrants who every day make significant contributions to this country, and DREAMers who were brought here as children and know no other home. We fight for them, too, because they are embedded in our society's fabric.

My heart filled with hope on that day, during a time when our nation was so deeply divided, as I watched coalitions form to fight for the right over our bodies, right to equal pay, right to feel safe in our communities, and basic human rights. As long as we are not alone in the fight, as long as we continue to link arms, we will have a chance in the struggle to achieve equality.

Hilda L. Solis, Board of Supervisors, Los Angeles County

To the men & women who are unafraid to show up, stand up…

You are THE RESISTANCE.

ACKNOWLEDGEMENTS

There are so many people and organizations that we would like to acknowledge; those who were instrumental in the success of the Women's March Los Angeles on January 21, 2017. We are very grateful for your participation in this historic event.

City of Los Angeles
Mayor of Los Angeles, Eric Garcetti
Supervisor Hilda L. Solis
Councilman Jose Huizar
Los Angeles City Hall
City of West Hollywood
Pershing Square
Center Staging
Neptunes Production
Grand Park. Los Angeles
City of Los Angeles, Permits Department, Special Events
Los Angeles Police Department
Los Angeles Fire Department
Los Angeles Department of Transportation
Los Angeles Department of Recreation & Parks
City of Los Angeles Bureau of Street Services
Medics on The Ball, EMT Services
SET Medics, LLC
SDM Security
A. Zelaya Security Services
LA Metro
LA Dash
Rally Bus
City of Los Angeles Bureau of Street Services
Roadway Construction

PREFACE

The largest Women's March in the world took place in Los Angeles on January 21, 2017. The peaceful and inspirational collaboration of more than 800,000 participants, speakers and performers did not happen without the tireless and selfless support of each and every person who gave of themselves to bring the March to life. This book is our heartfelt attempt to honor the volunteers who gave their time freely to help organize and execute our historic March, and to recognize and thank those who filled the streets of downtown LA in solidarity.

We knew it would be an emotional journey to gather the stories of those who participated. And it really was. We cried as we read the stories, laughed at some of the signs carried by the people who came together that day, and marveled at the love and trust in humanity that all who came brought with them. The day was empowering in a time when we needed, more than ever, to find our collective strength and community, and continues to fuel us as we move forward as the Women's March LA Foundation.

Our March was just one example worldwide of the positive change the combined strength that people aligned to a common purpose can bring to a city, a nation and our world. We hope that the images and stories in our book both remind you of the incredible day that was, and inspire you to make your voices heard going forward.

Together we are mighty. #hearourvoice.

Thank you from the bottom of our hearts,

Emi & Deena

For more information on how you can get involved with
Women's March LA Foundation go to www.womensmarchla.org.

INTRODUCTION

Why would 750,000 people of all genders, orientations, ages and backgrounds willingly and joyfully embrace unprecedented crowds, overburdened public transportation systems, threats of rain and hours on their feet? And, how did an idea that grew from a grassroots backyard conversation become an epic event that changed lives, flipped the narrative, and created a groundswell of peace, positivity, activism, inclusion, love and hope? The words and images of the Women's March Los Angeles: Hear Our Voice, Hear Our Story provide thoughtful, perceptive and visually stunning answers to these questions, and more.

In these pages, you will find the stories and faces of the broad spectrum of participants in the Women's March Los Angeles on January 21, 2017. You will understand the compelling reasons why we marched, how we marched and with whom we marched. You will see stories of inspiration and struggle, words of enlightenment and newfound activism are shared, images of families, of friends, and of strangers who became friends on that grand day on the streets of downtown Los Angeles.

The stories shared in the Women's March Los Angeles: Hear Our Voice, Hear Our Story will inspire you. The pictures will touch you where you live. For those who attended, the reminders of what many have recalled as one of the best days of their lives will inspire welcome memories and feelings to resurface. For those who were not able to attend in person, the generous sharing of stories and photographs will provide personal context to the narrative of an incredible worldwide movement that has only just begun.

Southern Californians showed up in record numbers to take their place on the right side of history. Our voices were heard. Women's March Los Angeles: Hear Our Voice, Hear Our Story documents the people, moments, ideas and energy that created this unprecedented day and inspires the work that remains to be done to guarantee the advancement and protection of speech, inclusion, diversity and human rights.

> "Our lives begin to end the day we become silent about things that matter."
> ~*Martin Luther King Jr.*

As an immigrant brought to this county illegally, I don't for one minute take for granted the opportunities this country has given me and my family.

Growing up poor in Chicago, as a child I knew that our power was our voice. My parents were involved in the community as that was the only way to stay safe.

We didn't have much but always knew we had to give back to the community.

My mom would always say "no tenemos mucho pero somos ricos."
(We don't have much but we are rich.)

How could we be rich? She said "we are rich in health, rich in friendships, rich as a community" My parents always believed that our community lifts us up when we are down.

After the election my heart hurt, I was devastated how could we as a society have voted for racism, misogyny, hate?

I started to organize the day after the election. I texted e-mailed and called everyone I knew. I needed to organize my community. I needed to make sense of what was going on. I then saw the Women's March on Washington Facebook page and communicated that I would be organizing a march in Los Angeles.

I needed to organize and bring myself to the table as I was afraid the Latino community would be left out, an after thought like every election.

Soon I became WE, we embarked on the planning of The Los Angeles Women's March. WE didn't know where it would go but we no longer felt powerless, voiceless. Our communities were coming together.

I marched for my community my family and especially for my Mother in law who I called mom. Mom was dying of stage-four cancer in my home as I was planning for the march.

Mom had sent in her ballot and said to me "Emi we are going to make history".

Mom died on Nov 30th and never made it to the march.

We made history, but not the way we expected to make history.

I will continue to organize; I will continue to fight for human rights because January 21st, 2017 showed the world what we can happen when we organize and unite our communities.

        Thank You,
        Emiliana Guereca
        Co-Executive Director
        Women's March Los Angeles Foundation

> Little did any of us know when we started this grassroots event what would transpire in the months ahead. For my part, the Women's March LA started the weekend after the election, over a tearful conversation in my backyard with my sisters, my daughter, my husband, my dad and my niece. We felt helpless and demoralized, wanting to effectuate change but feeling that our best intentions might not be enough. This little backyard dream grew into a movement that cannot be stopped. In Los Angeles we drew together 800,000 peaceful, passionate, empowered and inspired warriors of all genders, identities, orientations, nationalities, ages, religions and backgrounds. We marched, we celebrated, we learned, we embraced the power that was palpable that day, and I think it is accurate to say that all who participated that day had their lives changed forever.
>
> ~ Deena Katz

I remember seeing the Facebook post on the Women's March on Washington and for the first time since the presidential election I felt… hope.

I started making plans to go to D.C., but then I saw that Los Angeles was marching too. I knew then that I needed to participate here, LA was my home, and so I needed to figure out how I could get involved!

After much internet stalking, constant emailing, phone calling and general determination I managed to get myself on a volunteer phone call for the March! I was so excited! There were 50 of us on the line and I thought how amazing it was that this many people want to do this too…little did I know how that number would grow!

I helped the March with PR & Communications and on the historic day I arrived before dawn to get the credentials for press, media and VIPs set-up in Pershing Square, and organize my crew of volunteers. During that time, the Square had people making protest signs, and specifically I remember a woman who had created these beautiful paper banners in the shape of Phoenixes that were striking and symbolic. Busses started to arrive, people began to fill the area, and I got very emotional taking it all in. This, today, I thought, was what democracy looks like. I was so proud to be standing with what would turn out to be 750,000 amazing Angelinos, and many millions more around the world.

My daughter was just a little over a year old at the time when I first got involved with Women's March, and I volunteered in many ways for her. I want her to know that women are powerful forces and that her Mom was and is going to do whatever she can to make a better world for her. And to know that from ashes the Phoenix will always rise.

~ Ellen Crafts

It all started with a text. I, along with millions of others across the country, was in shock the night of November 8, 2016. It felt like I had been hit over the head with a brick; the energy all over California could be felt growing heavier and heavier as the night went on. I was texting with my boss, Emi, and neither of us could believe the state of existence we were suddenly in. The next day when we arrived at the office, it felt as if we were attending a funeral- and that's when I knew we wouldn't be able to sit back and just watch this happen- we needed to remind ourselves, our families and friends, and those across this country, that we stand for equality, love, patriotism, honesty, and integrity. Emi kept repeating how we needed to do something, we need to all come together, we need to march. She informed me of some groups organizing in Washington D.C., and she thought we needed to do the same here in Los Angeles. She applied for permits for the march that very same week in November.

From that day forward, we were inundated and overwhelmed with support and questions on how different groups could help, what the plan for January 21 was, how we could take action, what could be done. It's as if an anxious, restlessness energy for action and unity had been imposed on women and men of all ages across Southern California.

November to January was a blur; we had suddenly been tasked with organizing what would become one of the largest marches in the entire world. During those months, we didn't even have time to look up or catch our breath, as there was so much important work to be done. At times, it felt daunting, difficult, and as if a reprieve from it would never come. But then I was reminded of why this march, this movement, and this election meant so much to us. I believe every one of us has incredible women in our lives, who has always made the impossible look easy, who's work ethic, strength, dignity and compassion inspires us on a daily basis - for me, that was my boss, Emi, the Co-Executive Director of the WMLA organization, and my mother. I then realized Hillary Clinton reminded me of them both and her loss in the election had made me feel as though I had disappointed the most important women role models of my life.

That is why I organized, that is why I marched, and that is why January 21 felt absolutely surreal. Before even 8am that morning, I stood up on a ledge within Pershing Square to get a view of the streets, and was in total shock that the crowds had already filled the roads entirely. That's when it felt like I could finally exhale; the culmination of months of work, of 750,000 Angelenos making sure their voices were heard, and displaying peaceful unity and respect within our community, is the reason I am inspired to continue fighting each and every day.

~ Irene Aitkens

> "Give me your tired, your poor,
> Your huddled masses yearning to breathe free,
> The wretched refuse of your teeming shore.
> Send these, the homeless, tempest-tossed, to me:
> I lift my lamp beside the golden door."
> ~ Emma Lazarus

As I sat in my living room witnessing the events of Trumps presidency unfold in the most appalling manner, an indignant feeling overtook my body. I kept asking myself, 'what have we done?' Were the cries of Dr. King, S. B. Anthony, Chisholm and Malcom repressed again?

As a daughter of Muslim Iranian immigrants, I travelled a thousand miles to this country, welcomed by Lady Liberty to seek betterment in education and the right to exercise freedom under a constitution that built this great nation of refugees. Raised by a grandmother whose strength and courage was admired by the masses, a mother who taught me how to speak with gallantry and move about life independently, and my aunt whose love for her religion was my liberation and shaped my life I found myself afraid of what the future will hold. November 8th, when power was handed to a sexist whose anti Muslim and anti immigration rhetoric empowered the silenced voices of his zealot base was the day I began questioning the safety of my family, my unborn son's future, and it was then I knew that my silence would be a disfavor to the legacy of the women in my life and those in history who paved the way for me.

Eager to march in LA, closer to the event I reached out to the organizing committee to help and co-produced the "Why I March" video that became a segway to the stories of those women and men who marched.

~ Hanieh Jodat

"My story begins with my mother emigrating from Mexico into the United States when I was 3 years old, in hopes of being able to provide a better quality of life than the one I was living at the time. I spent most of my childhood with my grandmother, as she became my primary caretaker while my mom pursued the American Dream. My mother worked tirelessly for 6 years before she was finally able to earn enough money to pay for a "coyote" to have me safely cross the southern border and reunite with her. Since then, I have called Los Angeles my home.

In June 2012 President Obama announced DACA, and I remember feeling hopeful. That was the first time I felt like I would finally be able to have the opportunity to repay my mother and grandmother for their sacrifices. It felt like we had achieved the American Dream.

On November 8, 2016 I was ready to celebrate the first woman elected President in the history of the United States. As the night progressed however, the thought that maybe the improbable could become a reality started to become clearer. This was the moment I knew something needed to be done. The very next day Women's March LA started organizing, and there was no doubt in my mind that I had to be a part of it. Thus, I helped organize a safe logistics plan and worked with various organizations that joined the march. This, along with the work of all the other organizers brought over 750,000 people into the streets of DTLA to have our voices heard.

My contribution to this march was done to honor my mother and grandmother. Because they have sacrificed more than any other person has ever done so, in order for me to have an education, and opportunities to achieve any goal I set my mind to. After having lived through the march, I have regained that sense of hope I had prior to the election. My eyes have seen the people that stand along with me in the fight to protect basic human rights.

~ Karen Alvarado"

I sat alone in an AirBnb room in North Carolina on Election Night 2016. I felt totally alone, exhausted, and yet also completely connected to hundreds of people also feeling every emotion and running through a litany of questions in their mind. It was a heavy moment, but a moment I knew I could not stay in for long. I was eager to get home, back to my community, and around strong people, women in particular, who would energize and inspire me. In the months and weeks that followed, I felt the palpable energy of uprising, resistance, and that do-something attitude that was present everywhere. I was keenly aware that this was the moment of my generation where we could not remain silent; and every single voice mattered, including mine. Friends gathered over dinner, we met for organizing meetings in restaurants, museums, and backyards. We organized an art making party and were completely overwhelmed at the hundreds of people, of every kind, young and old, who showed up to create together. Creating together was a magical, messy process that pushed us to expand because shrinking was not an option.

I organized for love; love of my community, my country, and of people, friends or strangers, who deserve respect, dignity, and equality. I organized for my late grandmother whose very life was an act of resistance against oppression, racism, prejudice, and sexism that she faced every day. I organized for my mother and my father who have shown me that in order to make change, we have to get involved; no gains are made from the sidelines. I organized for children who will come in the next generations who will look through the lens of history and ask of all us who were present at this time, "and what did you do?" I organized because I had something contribute to the whole, and I most certainly believe we are stronger, better, and more effective when we work together.

~ Cristina Pacheco

" On January 21, 2017, I marched alongside numerous men, women, and children to fight for justice. With the recent events plaguing our country, as a photojournalist I have an obligation to capture hope in the midst of chaos. The community was marching for equality, marching against hatred and marching against division. A single frame of a photograph has the power to impact an individual so drastically that it can trigger immense change. Over the years as a country our ancestors have paved the way for progress and equal rights for all. Therefore, we must not reverse their efforts and must stand up and say no to the separation and hatred for the sake of future generations. Women are the cornerstone of our country and it is the responsibility of everyone to ensure their rights and safety. My hope is that the stories within my images will give rise to a social movement creating ambition and inspiration for change.

~ Chris Davidson "

"For most of history, Anonymous was a woman"

– *Virginia Woolf*

30 |

"If you are neutral in situations of injustice, you have chosen to side of the oppressor"

– *Desmond Tutu*

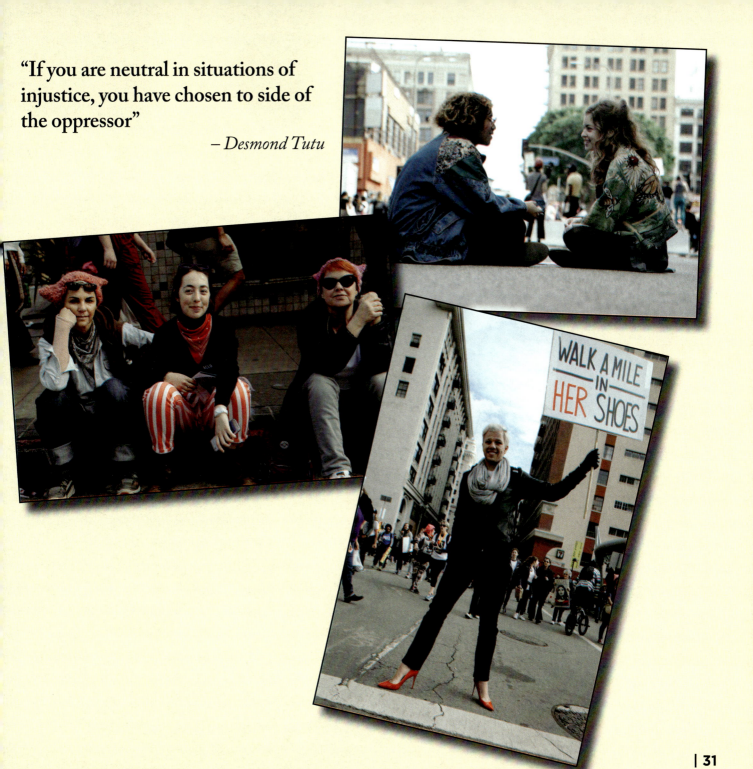

I am an immigrant from Mexico, I moved to the US 10 years ago. I am an Industrial Engineer that works on the Aerospace Industry, and I have also been a Flamenco dancer for 20 years now. I'm married to an incredible man and I have a beautiful daughter.

I decided to participate in this March because I have always been an advocate for human rights and equality for everyone, but the most important thing to me was to show my daughter that as a woman I have a voice, and she has a voice and has the right to fight for what is right. Many times at work or other places we get to see how sexist the environment can be for a woman, how your value gets determined not for what you know but by the way you look and because as a woman maybe they consider that you can't be smart enough or shouldn't have an opinion. I want to show her that she could do anything that she aspires to be, by always following the path of her passion, self-love and integrity. She will know by reading this book that her Mom stood not only for her rights but for the rights of millions of women that don't have a voice or feel they don't have a voice and will also know that women together can create the most amazing energy and can move mountains by supporting each other.

I know we are moving in the right direction, creating more value and strength for the next generation of women. Maybe my daughter will have the chance to march one day along with many other women, maybe we will do it together and if that happens it will mean that maybe… it still isn't good enough for women, but at least that will teach her that as women we have one of the most amazing skills or value that a women can have, and that is RESILIENCE, we never give up.

~ Claudia Flores

Morning light fell on crowds in Pershing Square. My friends--a therapist, a UN worker and a journalist--stayed close to avoid separation as marchers packed into the archway beneath the square's towering purple pillar. Embraced by the crowd, the incredulity, fear and defiance that brought me to the march were replaced by camaraderie, passion and humor.

In that squeezed passage, shared convictions took visual and auditory forms: Three pink pussy hats blazoned a diagonal across a bright orange wall. A spontaneous a cappella rendering of the Beatle's classic, Love, Love, Love brought five heads together—the graying wisps of an elderly woman, the thick brown and blond curls of younger crowns, and the dreads of a man who chimed in with the tones of the original brass chorus. Signs, hand-held overhead, entertained with caustic wit: "You Can't Comb over Racism & Sexism", "We are Not Ovaryacting", "I'm so Angry, I Made a Sign", "Stop Grabbing our Cats", "Equal Pay For Equal Work/Black Lives Matter/Love IS Love". A banner read, "Men of Quality Respect Women's Equality".

On the street, the parade widened and became denser. The final destination already full, eager marchers remained stationary. Bladders complained. A side detour was the only remedy.

A nearby building gave us grateful access to bathrooms and balcony. From this vantage the magnitude of the march was apparent: Blanketing every street and sidewalk, in trees, in carriages and in wheelchairs, the colors of the crowd were punctuated by splashes of pink. The crowd was powerful, gentle, and resistant. I learned later that the Women's Marches were the largest protest in American history—and at 750,000 strong in Los Angeles, we staged an unparalleled assembly.

The Declaration of Independence proclaims our right to pursue "Life, Liberty and the Pursuit of Happiness". I know that for women (and others), these aspirations are a work in progress. But the potential of many has flowered in universities, in a broadening workplace, in the home, and in our very souls.

~ Elizabeth Tracy

"I had been considering going to DC for the Women's March until I heard we would have one in Los Angeles. As a member of the Westchester-Playa Democratic Club, I asked others if they knew of a local group that would have a bus. Everyone had heard rumors, but no one had details.

I called the office of or City Councilman, Mike Bonin, and inquired. I was told, that it might be possible to get a bus. I went through all the paperwork, and sure enough, was told we could have a bus from our Councilman's Field office to and from the March. I told a few neighbors and Club members about it, and by word of mouth in a day or two the bus was full. Lots of communicating with riders, and we all met in Westchester on that beautiful sunny and chilly morning. There was so much energy among the 48 riders. It was a completely diverse group of all ages, genders and colors, from children to elderly, all with great signs. Some even made extra signs to share. On the way down we sang "I am Woman," discussed issues, and kept up the energy. Even the driver was excited.

When we arrived downtown, we split off into smaller groups and everyone had different experiences. It was exciting chatting with other participants, who came from everywhere and had wonderful signs, costumes, as we all shared the same convictions and shared experiences. There were a lot of Woman Power and anti-Trump sentiments. I felt like this was a gathering of the best of us. There were no incidents, it was friendly and it felt good, especially right after the inauguration, to make our voices heard. We were certainly stronger together, and will continue the fight.

~ Ellen Klein"

"A Feminist is anyone who recognizes the equality and full humanity of women and men"

– Gloria Steinem

"I am not a humanitarian,
I am a hell-raiser"
— *Mother Jones*

1/21/17: My mind is still reeling from what I witnessed today. The despair I felt from the Inauguration yesterday, washed away as soon as I arrived in Downtown L.A. Pam, (my partner of 17 years) and I wanted - needed to be there, not only to represent our LGBTQ Community, but for women everywhere and in history, who had paved the way for us and our rights, and to be present for those that couldn't be there also.

In Pershing Square, we became enveloped by thousands of people, from all walks of life, and then thousands more. I couldn't believe the sight of it, the sheer scale of humanity all in one place. The crowd was so thick, the concern of violence or riots breaking out crossed my mind. But no, it was PEACEFUL, it was loving, as if everyone there was feeling the same thing, realizing that they too were becoming a part of history in the making. It was like a true 'United State of America'. This was much more than a protest, or a march, it was a call for unity and an unbridled show of our democracy in action.

I snapped the selfie above of Pam and I at the Women's March L.A.: A day that I will never forget.

This energy doesn't lie. It only grows in truth. Something has been awoken. Whether we stand alone, or in the masses, our voices have been unleashed, and that holds more infinite power than division or hate.

~ Gina Acuña

Joan Abend & Sylvia de la Sancha: Friends for over 30 years

I marched for the sake of all girls who were too young to do so like my two grandgirls, Avenay Isabelle and Amalia Joy. As long as I am alive, I refuse to sit still and see their futures diminish. Like all Americans, they deserve a fair and just country and one in which women and minorities are treated equal. ~Sylvia de la Sancha

Participating in this march provided a powerful and positive way to support women, diversity and equal rights for all of us at a time in this country when so many things were and are being undermined. Standing together we can make a difference and challenge the status quo.

~ Joan Abend

I will never forget standing side by side with my friends and family in a sea of like minded people, seven hundred and fifty thousand strong. Not to mention the millions of other people marching around the world. We will rise up and resist until...

IN OUR AMERICA

WOMEN ARE IN CHARGE OF THEIR OWN BODIES.

SCIENCE IS REAL.

EDUCATION IS PARAMOUNT.

BLACK LIVES MATTER.

DIVERSITY IS CELEBRATED.

KINDNESS IS EVERYTHING.

LOVE IS LOVE.

~ Camryn Manheim

On January 21, 2017, I saw the resistance rise. The Women's March was more than just 750,000 people in Los Angeles alone but rather an accumulation of people marching to fight for the hope and dream of what is still to come.

At the march, we went from "I" to "We." We became part of something that we will never be able to understand. If that isn't G-d, I do not know what else it would be. While November 8 had me questioning my faith, January 21 brought it back full force.

The night before the march, I was with three of my closest friends. We laughed, we cried, we shared in the love that we have for this country and most importantly, the love we have for each other. Falling asleep that night, the following quote kept me awake. I didn't understand why until I got home after the march. The quote is:

The Devil whispered in my ear,

"You're not strong enough to withstand the storm."

Today I whispered in the Devil's ear,

"I am the storm."

While I believe the quote is perfect as it is, the only thing that I'd change is that on January 21, "I" didn't just whisper in the Devil's ear, "We" did.

~ John Erickson

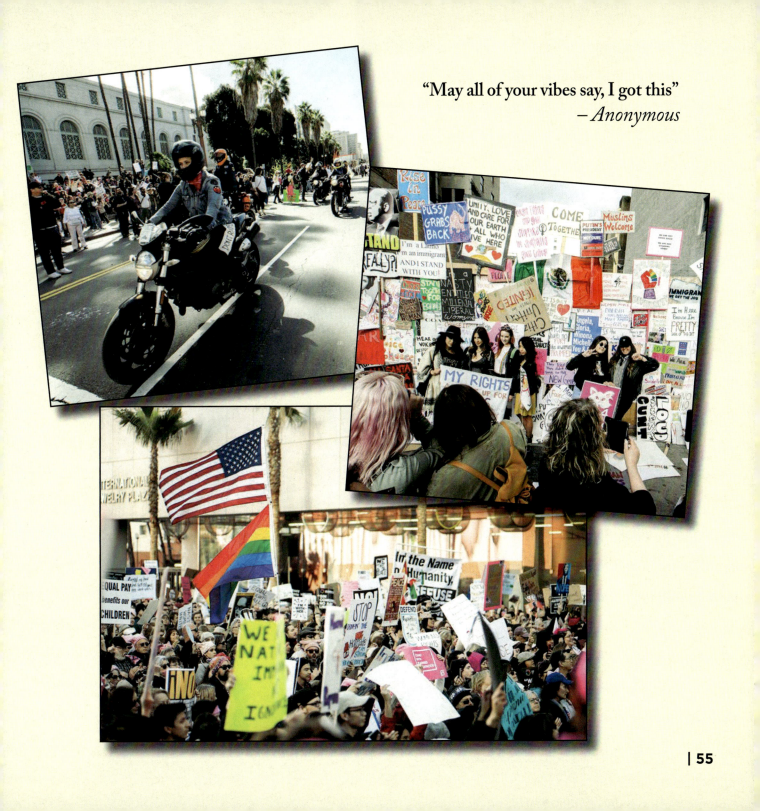

"May all of your vibes say, I got this"
– *Anonymous*

" I am truly grateful to have had the experience walking in the March with my husband and 2 sons, Forrest and Truman. Forrest is 18 and has high functioning autism. Truman is 16 and is a budding graphic designer and artist. My husband and I do architecture and have an office in Pershing Square.

In preparation for the event, I had talked to Forrest about what to expect over and over for days, to "set him up" for anything that might occur. Needless to say the day was fantastic and all went well. My greatest memory was hearing my sons chime back, "Her Body her Choice" as we were marching down Hill Street towards Grant Park, to my, "My Body my Choice".

I know my sons will grow up more sensitive to women's issues and help pave the way to a better tomorrow.

Thank you for arranging the event and I look forward to many more.

~ Kim Lesak "

" I am not an activist. I donate to my charities, volunteer and vote diligently, but never marched or rallied before, and certainly never organized a protest! Then on November 8th of 2016 that all changed. Mr. Trump's apocalyptic vision of America included turning our backs on climate change, limiting women's reproductive rights, persecuting my Muslim friends, and building a wall against our neighbors. I couldn't imagine this new America, and felt frightened for my child. So I joined a group of women I'd never met, to do a job I've never done. I did it unpaid, in between full time work and parenting. And hundreds of others did too. We all did our part to pull together an event that people could safely and peacefully attend, to show their unity and support for each other. We expected 100k people to come to the LA Women's March. Instead I stood up for the America I know and love with 750,000 of my closest friends.

~ Liz Love "

We are the Asian Pacific American Women Lawyers Alliance. We made the decision to join the Women's March and to march together as women lawyers of color in solidarity with others who oppose the racist, sexist, xenophobic campaign of Donald Trump. We are deeply committed to defending the gains of the historic Women's Movement and we felt that it was very important to take to the streets in a very visible, vocal and angry demonstration of our discontent. There was no mistaking the anti-woman tone of Trump's comments about how he believes women should be treated. He boasted about sexually assaulting women and treating them like sex objects to be valued solely by their attractiveness to him. His lack of respect for women was vividly evident in his debates with Hillary Clinton wherein he attempted to intimidate, bully and belittle based upon her gender. And his bigotry extended beyond women, to Mexicans whom he described as drug runners and rapists, to the judge sitting on one of his many cases whom he cast aspersions upon because of his Mexican American heritage, to the Muslims whom he promised to keep out of our country, to the disabled reporter whom he mocked then denied that he had done that. We marched to protest the regressive right-wing policies which Trump is advancing against America. We marched and we will continue to march, advocate and agitate until this illegitimate presidency is relegated to the dustbin of history.

~ Mia Yamamoto

The night of November 7th was a dark night of the soul for me – as an environmentalist, as a feminist, and as an American.

As my fellow Americans elected a president whose pro-polluter agenda threatens the health of our communities and our children, I knew we had to take to the streets and demand that the voices of the majority of our population—women—are heard. But it wasn't just women that I marched for – it was for all of the oppressed and marginalized people for whom Trump promised to make life much harder; for the people whose lives and livelihoods he openly threatened.

Women, low-income communities, and people of color frequently bear the heaviest burdens from climate change and industrial pollution. These communities face a greater risk of getting sick, losing their livelihoods, living in poverty, and being displaced when weather disasters strike.

Environmental issues ARE economic issues. Environmental issues ARE health issues. Environmental issues ARE justice and equity issues. And environmental issues ARE women's issues. As an environmentalist, it was important for me to spread the message that a healthy environment is a basic right for all of us - regardless of where we live, how we vote, or what we look like; and that I won't stand idly by while this administration puts corporate polluters and profits before people.

The mothers of Flint, Michigan and the women and youth leaders of the Standing Rock Sioux were the first ones in their communities to stand up for climate justice. We must amplify their voices and continue the fight to protect our families' futures and ensure our essential rights to clean air, clean water, and healthy communities.

My voice will be among those voices making these demands. My feet will be firmly planted on the frontlines.

The Women's March in Los Angeles was a pivotal rallying point for many and I look forward to seeing what we can accomplish together.

~ Natural Resources Defense Council

GIRLS JUST WANNA HAVE FUNDING for PLANNED PARENTHOOD

WELL BEHAVED WOMEN RARELY MAKE HISTORY

" My daughter Sofia Laila Puentes who is 9 years old and I, Paola Rojas Puentes attended the women's March in Los Angeles on 1/21/17. I immigrated from Colombia when I was 9 years old, now our lives have come full circle and my daughter is the same age I was when my mother brought me to this amazing country, escaping an abusive relationship, leaving behind all our family and two classes shy of completing her law degree, so that she & I could have a better opportunity. I wanted my daughter to be part of the march because it's important for her to understand the struggles of women & immigrants, that we are lucky to live here where the rule of law and changes to the laws are enforced and protected and also that we need to stand up when others try to diminish our rights. We marched in solidarity with all women and all immigrants that make the very bones & veins of this wonderful country.

~ Paula Puentes "

As an American Muslim of South Asian origin, I have read and been exposed to many forms of activism. One that holds close to my heart is the Salt March. Gandhi's vision was that we must be prepared to physically give our bodies to the cause. The Women's March embodied such a deep value and was a great beginning, a call to action.

The Women's March spoke to my heart. The sea of people who gathered was a testimony for the voices that were marginalized and unheard in our country. It spoke to the hunger in us all for a just, fair world. It also showcased the magnificent power of women, to come together for a cause.

January 21st, my 17 year old son and I left home with ample time to get to the march. The number of people who were there and still flowing in was nothing I had predicted. As I waded in through the crowds towards the podium I marveled at the knowing that so many people cared.

My message was simple but clear. As an American Muslim we are living in very challenging times. The vicarious liability imposed on American Muslims to take ownership for violent terrorism carried out by terrorists everywhere is unreasonable and wrong. Pew Research Center estimates that there were about 3.3 million Muslims of all ages living in the United States in 2015. This means that Muslims made up about 1% of the total U.S. population (about 322 million people in 2015) and we estimate that that share will double by 2050.

When Dr. King marched in Washington (1963) in his famous I have a Dream Speech he said that he was there today, "To dramatize a shameful condition. In a sense we have come to our nation's capital to cash a check, returned with insufficient funds."

And as I spoke to the thousand gathered that day I said, "We are here today not to cash a check but to withdraw the funds that we have all deposited."

~ Soraya Dean

I'm an extreme advocate for women's rights, equality, and ultimately the empowerment of women around the world. Yes, I'm a man, but in my heart is the need to inspire and empower women to, "Go Beyond!". With that said, I'm extremely proud to have been a lead volunteer of the women's march and honored to work directly with Emi. This event along with the leadership of Emi, hugely impacted my life and set me on clearer course in life.

I think it's interesting to start from the beginning. So here it is. One day I was looking for women groups to support and in one of those searches popped up, "Women's March LA". I was like cool a march to celebrate women. As I researched more, I saw that this was so much more than just a celebration, but a movement. At the time, I didn't know how big it was as I'd never heard much about it. Needless to say, I was persistent over a course of two weeks to connect with someone to volunteer. Thank God, I was given the opportunity to help.

I felt like I was part of something that was bigger than me. I'd found my calling. From The energy in the air to the comradely to the love and the relationships forged; It was absolutely amazing. It was also nice getting the kisses on the cheeks from a few of the grandmothers who thanked me for being a man...showing up for women.

The love was intoxicating. The hugs. The high 5's. The faces. The smiles. The mission. The movement...will never be forgotten.

~ Terry Briggs

> I marched as a granddaughter, daughter, a mother, and a wife.
>
> I marched because as a mother of two boys, I want them to grow up in a world where women are treated, paid, respected and loved as an equal.
>
> I marched because I am hopeful this current moment in our country will not divide us but unite us as it did on this day.
>
> I marched because I'm a woman.
>
> ~Rene Wang Brown

"After the election I was so distraught. I had this deep sadness. I couldn't believe that I lived in a country that could elect this man. What did that say about us? I wanted to pack up and leave. When I came home election night I saw my boys; these two wonderful boys who deserve so much better than this. If I ran away, what would I be teaching them? I have always tried to teach them to have a voice and to help those in need. But my question to myself was "How"? I did not know.

I met with friends the next day and talked with faraway friends on Facebook. There was a need for connection to make sense of this. Then a friend messaged me. He said, "You walk the walk everyday of your life. You are a shining example of what is good on this earth. What is infinite is what you already have in abundance; knowledge, acceptance, hope and love. It is what will prevail."

This brought tears to my eyes. This friend stood to lose so much more than I did. He could lose his right to openly love, but he thought about me. This is who we are; we look out for each other. At that moment I decided I had to do something.

I saw a conversation about a Women's March on Washington and ended up chatting with a few women about doing one in L.A. It really is a blur. We knew nothing about each other except that we were in this together. We promoted the march, responded to posts and messages, gathered volunteers and explored partnerships.

The day of the march was one of the most profound days of my life, seeing not only Los Angeles, but the world coming together in solidarity. It was overwhelming. No words could ever describe it. Then finding my family among the 800k people and seeing my sons face. Knowing that he sees that there is still so much goodness in the world. That one person can make a difference.

~ Tracy Samson

"It doesn't matter who is at the top, it matters what we do at the bottom"
– *Eric Garcetti*

> I marched because, as a lesbian woman, I knew President Trump's rise to power gave a permission slip to attack marginalized groups and has put many American lives and civil rights in danger. As the President of GLAAD, I wake up every morning to ensure that underrepresented people have a voice. That task can feel enormous but the millions of people marching on that day made me realize that we have an army ready to fight for humanity.
>
> ~ Sarah Kate Ellis
> President & CEO,
> GLAAD

As soon as I heard about the Women's March, I knew I had to participate. Like many people, I was feeling dejected, depressed and powerless after the election. I have never participated in any march, any political action or demonstration.

I was surprised in the weeks leading up to the March, how many people I encountered that didn't know about it. This was especially true of the younger women I know who are under 30. It became my mission to let everyone I knew, every stranger I met, know about the march and inviting them.

The words of one of my favorite songwriters, Billy Bragg, kept coming to mind. He often says that the biggest enemy of all to those of us that want a better world is actually cynicism; our own cynicism that nothing will ever change. The Women's March LA embodied this spirit and solidified for me that I must keep fighting and fighting the voice inside that says to give up.

~ Susan Bauer

"The march was earthshattering for me in so many ways. I saw the strength of love, in action, magnified by more people than I've ever seen in my life, together- unified in purpose. I got on the train headed to downtown in South Pasadena. I had decided to come without my 5 year-old daughter, Audrey Lucia in case violence erupted; my husband stayed home with her. Waiting on the subway platform waiting for my friend near Union Station, I saw this sea of humanity just pour out, train after train after train. I was in awe of our numbers, and of the strength and joyfulness that was so undeniably palpable. When I called my husband to excitedly describe what I was seeing, he decided in that moment to meet me there, with Audrey in tow. I am so grateful they made it! Together we marched. I wanted to show Audrey that she can do anything, and be anything she wants; to stand up for what she believes in. I marched for the right of my brother and everyone else to marry the people they love, without boundaries, without fear. I am incredibly proud to have been a part of the March with my little family. So proud to be a part of this movement.

Thanks again for the opportunity to tell our story!

~ Sylvia, Audrey and Ray Pabon"

SHIELD AGAINST Racism & Sexism

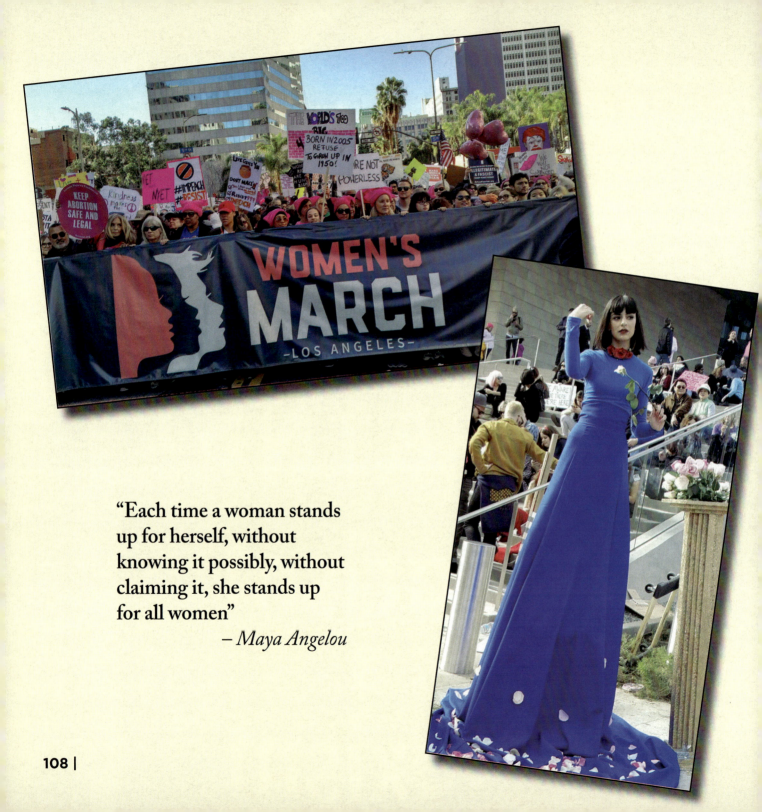

"Each time a woman stands up for herself, without knowing it possibly, without claiming it, she stands up for all women"
— *Maya Angelou*

I was out of the country on November 8, 2016, but was able to follow the election results as they were happening. My sense of dread and fear increased as the evening went on, the pit in my stomach deepened, and then the unbelievable happened. It was surreal not being in the United States when Trump was elected. I equate it to my experience on September 11, 2001, when I was in Yellowstone National Park on a photography workshop, far from my supportive circle of family and friends, devastated and angry.

When the Women's March in Washington, DC was announced, I started to make plans to travel east. When it became apparent that marches would be taking place throughout the country, as a native Los Angeleno, I wanted to march in my city. I wanted to be part of the resistance to an incoming administration that was already demonstrating its' opposition to women's rights, the rights of immigrants, LGBTQ rights as well as displaying early signs of fascism and racism. My oldest daughter, Chelsea, would march with me here and my two younger daughters, Lauren and Allie would march in San Diego.

We arrived early at the corner of 5th and Hill so we could join in at the "beginning" of the march. It quickly became evident as all streets in the area became packed that there was no official starting point. We just started moving slowly and peacefully, chanting, singing, dancing, hoping, praying that our sheer numbers would show the world what our city and country truly stands for.

My photos don't document anger or hate or evil intent. They document a peaceful, yet passionate demand for all human rights by a quarter of a million women, men and children. And those signs! The resistance most definitely has a sharp sense of humor.

~ Kathi Mangel

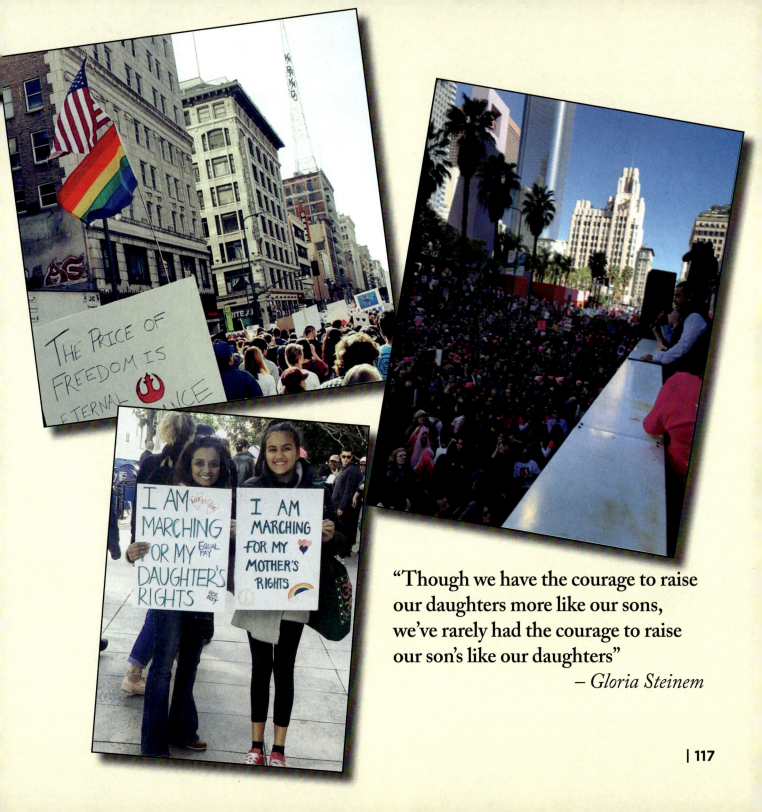

"Though we have the courage to raise our daughters more like our sons, we've rarely had the courage to raise our son's like our daughters"
– Gloria Steinem

| 117

As a woman of color, I am deeply concerned about the state of our nation. I'm not usually an activist in the streets, but upon the election of 45, I jumped into action. I'm from the business community and my many years of experience have taught me how to build teams and motivate others.

So for the Los Angeles Women's March, I organized nine other friends to join me to create our own contingent. My partner would be attending the March in Washington, but together we worked on our signage and slogans for DC and Los Angeles. The New York Light Brigade made my illuminated HANDS OFF! Sign. With 45 in the White House, it seemed perfect to tell him to keep his Hands Off! Our Bodies and Our Rights.

~ Melinda White

"We marched. We marched for our grandmothers who came before us and for our grandchildren that have yet to come. We marched forward in the hope that our once great country will go with us instead of turning backwards to a time when we had very few rights, if any at all. We marched."

We had a blast! I drove down to Los Angeles from San Luis Obispo to join up with my twin sister, Andrea, and her husband, Chris. We woke at the ass-crack of dawn on Saturday, January 21st and jumped on the freeway heading towards downtown. Passing and being passed by carloads of pink pussy-hatted ladies, we honked and waved our way to Pershing Square.

Having got there nice and early, we were able to find good, cheap parking just blocks from the march. Meeting up with the crowd was such an overwhelmingly positive feeling, it was like being high. (When they go low, we go high!) We quickly dispersed the few extra hats we had to bare-headed men, women and children, then we joined the crowd listening to speeches being given by the likes of Jane Fonda, Barbara Streisand and Miley Cyrus, to name a few.

As we moved down the avenue we were treated to the awesome sounds of The Edge and Juliette Lewis singing "In the Name of Love". WoW! As we joined the end of the march and paraded to city hall, we thanked our lucky stars that we were being enveloped by the magnanimous karma of hundreds of thousand like-minded, kind-hearted, intelligent progressives left-wing resistors!

Then we left, drove as far away from the crowd as we could get and went bowling. What a perfect day!

~ Yvonne Helmes

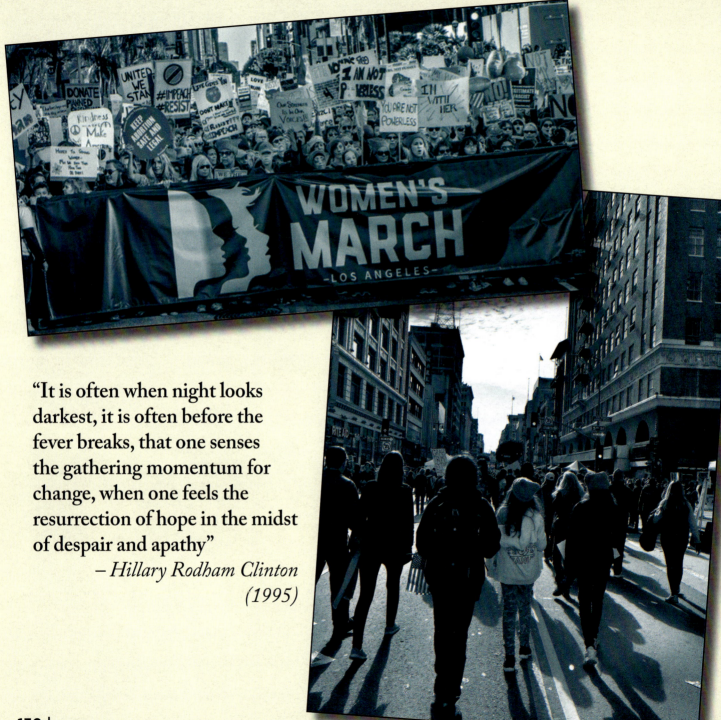

"It is often when night looks darkest, it is often before the fever breaks, that one senses the gathering momentum for change, when one feels the resurrection of hope in the midst of despair and apathy"
— *Hillary Rodham Clinton (1995)*

"What are those?" I said to a tall woman. I was referring to the floppy lumps of extra fabric on either side of the pink knit beanie she wore. Pink buds spouted from her head.

It was 7:00am and the parking lot at the metro station in Redondo Beach was already filling up. When I asked Bill to join me for the Women's March he expressed his concerns. "What if enough people don't show up?" He didn't want the march to be made fun of or denigrated. "And I don't want to be the only man."

We were both happy to see so many women at the station. Women waited by cars. They stood in groups, talked, laughed, sipped Starbucks and smoothies. Some women carried signs. Some held the hands of young girls. One woman pushed a baby carriage, her young son by her side. There were old women and young women and women of all different colors, shapes and sizes. Some women were with men.

Bill and I made our way up the stairs to the platform where there were more Pink PussyHats waiting for the next train. At each stop Pink PussyHats got on the train.

"I bet this train has never been this full on a Saturday," I said to Bill The train was filled with pink. Women stood by the doors. They huddled in groups of twos and threes and more. Some women were with men. Their voices hummed and swirled through the car. I could feel the throb of purpose and intent thick in the air. In my belly I felt a tingle, a mixture of anticipation, nervousness, excitement, hope. I was stretching beyond my casing.

I thought how significant it was, me on a train filled with women in Pink PussyHats on my way to a woman's march. And of course I didn't know at the time how historic the march would be. That I'd be marching in solidarity with millions of women in 500 cities and onehundred countries. All I knew was that I was on a pink train headed downtown and a spark had ignited in my belly.

"This feels significant," I said and threaded my fingers through Bill's. "Me and all these women, it's amazing. I think something important is happening here."

~ Carolyn Ziel

Three perspectives on "My mom and I marched so my daughter hopefully won't have to in the future."

Grandma: The goal was to bond with my daughter, her friends, and all the marchers in our frustration, anger, disbelief of the election. The immediate result was the shock to see and be with so many upbeat, encouraging women and men, the saddest was to see a woman, my age, with a sign: I cannot believe I am doing this shit again. The overall takeaway was the amazing realization that this was worldwide: not just big cities, but tiny towns, throughout the world. The sisterhood marches on. Today it is impossible to remember how exactly the world / the US stood news-wise in Jan. So much more has happened, so much worse. My exhaustion and my dread occasionally are lifted as I recall the camaraderie in the LA streets, where no movement was possible in the jam packed streets.

Mom: After the election I was in a state of paralysis – to have lived forty years in what I thought was a progressive society and yet, underneath, it wasn't really. Sure, in the STEM fields we make less than our male colleagues on average, and sure, I've dealt with casual sexism on a fairly regular basis – but we were improving! We were on an upward trajectory! Now I worry for my daughter's rights – to fully express herself, be herself, and be able to make decisions for herself. The march definitely helped – it was overwhelming and positive and so packed that we only made it one block in 3 hours.

Daughter: (she's 2 – just thought the matching sparkly t-shirt was cool!)

~ Stephanie Rasmussen

> I went to the Women's March because I needed to be surrounded by likeminded people who were willing to stand up to bigotry, misogyny, anti-Semitism and homophobia.
>
> I saw this beautiful young woman and told her she reminded me of the girl in the poster. She was so honored to pose for me. After sharing the photo on Facebook, I learned that I was already friends with her father on Facebook. Los Angeles suddenly became a small town at that moment.
>
> And, of course, her name was Grace...
>
> ~ Tish Laemmle

"I didn't succumb to the stereotype that science wasn't for girls"
— NASA Astronaut, Sally Ride

I spent a lifetime watching others fight for Women's Rights, then 45 took over. I felt helpless. His was stripping away all of our protections & rights.

Marching in the Women's March was the start of my empowerment. So many Women & Children & Husbands & Friends were there supporting what is right.

I can't sit back any longer. I have changed.

I am "woke."

RESIST!

~ Denise Pleune

"Women who seek to be equal with men lack ambition"
— *Timothy Leary*

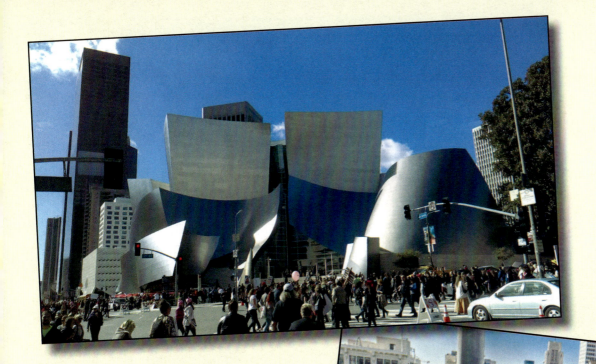

"All men should be feminist. If men care about women's rights, the world will be a better place. We are all better off when women are empowered. It leads to a better society."
— *John Legend*

On November 9th, I woke up and hoped that it was a bad dream. That hope was dashed on the rocks of the morning news. As I went through my morning routine I struggled to find my emotional footing in this new and unimaginable reality. Maybe the exhaustion from staying up late to watch the election coverage was making me emotional. Undoubtedly it was bad --very bad --but was it really catastrophic? After all, I'd lived through other presidential elections that didn't go the way I wanted and the world didn't come to an end. But, I knew in my heart that this was different. I got in the car, and as I pulled away from the curb and headed for the office I cried.

As time went by, moving inexorably toward Inauguration Day, the shock and grief were replaced by alternating bouts of denial and anger. I've always been an optimistic and solutions-oriented person, but I felt powerless. I made donations to organizations that protect women's rights, the environment, immigrants' rights and press freedom, but still I felt untethered and adrift. I remember the moment I saw the Facebook post about the L. A. Women's March. Finally, there was an action I could take to stand up and show my opposition to what was happening. I knew nothing would stop me from being there.

I got to Pershing Square early, and within the hour the streets of DTLA were filled with hundreds of thousands of people. L.A. is a city with physical characteristics that usually keep people isolated in their own cars, in their own neighborhoods, in their own realities. The sprawl of this city works against people coming together and connecting. Not on this day. It may have been a Women's March, but what distinguished this event was its inclusiveness. People of every demographic were welcome and welcoming. Women and men, gay and straight, seniors and children, students, white-collar professionals, union members, hipsters, suburban soccer moms with babies in strollers, artists, people in wheelchairs, skateboarders, activists and people who had previously considered themselves apolitical showed up. Strangers exchanged smiles and encouraging words. And, putting aside our personal preoccupations, we all came together to say: No! We won't stand for this! This is not who we are. And, on that day, I realized that although the struggle might be long and at times discouraging, it was far from hopeless.

~ Lisa Dee

"I am woman, hear me roar"
— *Helen Reddy*

"I marched with my mom on what would have been her own mother's 92nd birthday. What should have been a 30 minute ride downtown on the Metro took us close to three hours because all the trains were too packed to let anyone in. (We were at the second stop on the line.) We finally ended up squeezing into a train going the wrong direction and staying on, which eventually looped us back to downtown. It was so impossible to get on the metro going towards downtown that 100 or so people ended up starting their own march in North Hollywood (the opposite terminus of the line) because they couldn't get on a train.

The march itself was absolute madness. The craziest part was seeing the cars on the streets that hadn't gotten blocked off that were just trapped in a sea of people. (Remember, 70k people were expected, but 750k showed up). I have never seen so many people happily walking in LA. I only encountered two Men's Rights Activists shouting at us during the march, and one man in full MAGA regalia standing outside city hall. Everyone else was there in solidarity. It was incredibly heartening to be part of this sea of people, united in our belief that it was not only our constitutional right to voice our dissent, but our duty to speak out against someone we see as a fundamental threat to anyone who is not a wealthy/cis/hetero/white male. I marched because as a white woman, it is my duty to show up, flex my privilege, and be the best ally/accomplice I can be.

On the train ride back, I got to explain to two little girls (maybe 9 and 11 years old) and their mother the significance of the hand knit pussy hats that an unknown to them marcher had given them when she couldn't find the friends she brought them for. I got to explain that they were wearing art and history. That fiber artists worldwide had been making these hats for months for friends, family, and marchers across the country, and there had been a nationwide shortage of pink yarn as a result. That they were called "Pussy Hats" as a way of reclaiming the language used by our President* to demean women. I know that moment had a profound impact on their mom- I hope they will remember it too.

~ Emily Leher

> Me decide llegar como voluntaria cuando mi hija me lo pido. Me traje a mi esposo y hijos como voluntarios para la marcha.
>
> Yo soy taquera de oficio. Tengo 40 anos en los Estados Unidos la vida no a sido facil para mi y mis hijos pero trabajamos duro, le echamos ganas.
>
> Estoy de voluntaria para ensenarle a mis hijos que valemos halgo, que somos mas que illegales somos humanos y merecemos mas de lo que tenemos.
>
> Lo volveria a hacer fue una experencia fenomenal para mi y mi familia. Estamos orgullosos de aver participado

> I decided to participate as a volunteer when my daughter asked me. I brought my husband and kids as volunteers. I am a taco prep Cook by trade.
>
> I have been in the United States for 40 years and life has not been easy for me and my kids but we work and we put forth the effort.
>
> I am a volunteer to show my kids we are worth it, we are more than just illegals we are human beings and deserve more than what we have.
>
> I would do this again the experience was phenomenal for me and my family. We are proud to have participated.
>
> ~ Liduvina Padilla Galvez

> I am a first-generation Latina who, had it not been for my parents emigrating from Mexico, I would not have had the opportunities that I have fought for, tooth and nail, to accomplish and to "pay it forward" to others who come after me. I believe that ALL AMERICANS, regardless of color, race, creed, have the right to pursue their dreams. My parent's dream was to live a righteous life and spread the dream of hope to their children. We come from a family of flaws and strengths, just like any other family. But, we want everyone to have that right to pursue THAT AMERICAN DREAM.
>
> My hope is that I will be able to give back in supporting others in their professional and personal pursuits. And, as my parents taught me, race, color, creed is irrelevant. So, on that day, I walked proudly and peacefully with my sister and with my aunt. In my heart, I felt like I represented all of the women that came before me, and all of the women who are to come after me. It was a walk that represented equality, justice and freedom.
>
> It was a walk that represented all of my younger-aged clients who have suffered traumas in their lives and want to overcome their traumas to live a rewarding life. It was a walk that represented the Master's students that I have taught who are in pursuit of a professional achievement. It was a walk that represented all of my colleagues who share that same desire of helping others, just as I do. And, finally, it was a walk that represented all of the women in my family. I know that they would have been very proud of us walking to represent countless others who want to be able to live in a land of justice, freedom and liberty.
>
> And, if that meant that I had to walk in the hot sun proclaiming these rights and protesting an indignant and an unruly man who sits in the office of the President, then I had to do it. And, if I have to keep marching again, I will do it. Many women have marched before us and we will not go calmly into that good night. As John Paul Jones said, "We have not yet begun to fight". And, we will fight with words, peaceful marches and with the law on our side. Justice shall prevail!
>
> ~ Maria Gengenbacher

"At 7:45 AM on January 21, I was with my friend Mary in a long ticket line at the Pasadena's Sierra Madre Station. Not many people carried protest signs, and I felt a little embarrassed with our group of three juggling 18 handmade signs that kept slipping off.

Forty five minutes later the line had hardly moved.

"Why can't someone collect cash and buy hundreds of tickets at a time?" The lady in front of us asked, visibly upset. "It would surely expedite things."

"There are no paper tickets," Mary explained. She pulled out a tap card from her purse. "Take mine. I'll have to buy tickets with my friend here anyway."

Her generosity seemed to embarrass the stranger. "How much do I owe you?"

Mary didn't know how much was left on her card, and there wasn't time to figure it out. "Go catch your train and march," she said, pushing the other away. After a while, she told me, "Forget the tickets. Follow me," then sped off. By the time I caught up to her, Mary was already on the other side of the turnstile. For a second I hesitated, but since the word "Tap" was clearly printed, I dutifully obeyed the command and touched the word with my hand, hoping for the same magic that had sent Mary to the other side. Nope! Nothing. So I did an aerial ballet split and hop across the barrier. My first *public* act of civil disobedience was a success.

We each claimed a protest sign, and the rest were given out to whoever wanted them. We were like one giant family, all itching to march, but miles and miles separated us from the main event, and it didn't look like we would get there soon, if ever.

Union Station, finally.

We belonged in history. I belonged in history, me, who arrived here empty-handed, without English. At an estimated 4.6 million worldwide, the Women's March turned out to be the largest in the history of the United States.

Women rule.

Words rule—their significance in communication, their cadence when chanted by the millions, their poignancy in brief, cutting messages, their power to inform, to reveal, to shift point of view, to explode like a bomb in the face of enemies, to empower, to lift and give voice, to demand, to tear down, to take back, to unite and amplify one's cause."

~ Hong-My Basrai

THANK YOU, MOM

for teaching me

MARGARET CELESTINE O'NEIL MORTIMORE

LOVE
COURAGE
+
RESPECT

♥ ALWAYS overcomes hate

> I, too, am an immigrant. I too made this place my home.
>
> As a photojournalist I felt compelled to take part and document this little slice of American History.
>
> It was indeed an unusual scene to see the Downtown L.A. streets flooded with people of all ages and color.
>
> A special day where we were all one: smiles, handshakes, chants and a feeling of hope and change.
>
> This is America.
>
> This is the America that got us to leave our hometowns to be part of a collective dream.
>
> The America that doesn't discriminate and stands up for injustice.
>
> Let's keep the dream alive.
>
> ~ Alessandro Elena

Since November I felt paralyzed. The tears I was too tired to shed seeped directly into my muscles and hardened. I was voiceless. My words stuffed somewhere down my throat. Irretrievable. But then the marched happened. And as I emerged from the subway tunnel with my daughters' hands in mine, something happened.
I found my voice again.
We smiled at every stranger (for just being there meant we weren't strangers anymore).
We held our sign high.
Promises etched into my brain as I walked through the streets.
I promise to stay involved.
I promise to treat others with kindness.
I promise to call my representatives when I feel civil rights are being violated.
I promise I will not stop. I promise to listen. I promise to keep going. Always.
I recommit to my own writing because books teach empathy.
The numbers in Pershing Square overwhelmed me. Showing up in numbers matters. It makes a statement no matter how anyone tries to spin it. And the camaraderie is builds is palpable. I realized we needed this togetherness. And I also realized people are seriously awesome at making signs.
I march to make people pay attention and I march to know I'm are not alone.
I marched for my daughters.
I marched for my grandmothers.
I marched with my mom at my side.
I marched because as an artist it is my job to speak out.
I marched in solidarity with every person on this planet that is marginalized. (And I'll say it again. I promise to listen.)
I promise to remember when they gaslight us:
Zero arrests were made
We were 750,000 strong.
Being there felt like love and connectedness. It lifted the darkness. It built hope. It felt as good as it did when my mom held me after I broke my wrist in grade school.
Remember the peace.
Remember we are not weak because we care about human rights.

Because the truth is, you can try and divide us but you will only bring us closer together. That is America to me.
Right now, the future leaders of our country, the ones who will bring positive change are listening and are being fueled by this movement. This is happening now. They are emboldened because we marched.

I needed this fuel.

Yesterday we cried. Today we marched. Tomorrow we act.

~ Beth Navarro

"In late November I had become extremely vocal on social media about my advocacy for women's rights and gender equality. I was struggling to stay engaged at my full time job while feeling the gut wrenching pains of injustice occurring everyday in our country. Although I found some comfort in conversations I was partaking in on social media, I needed more. Que a serendipitous conversation I shared with a former work colleague who reached out to me with news about a group of women organizing a march in Northern California. At first I was hesitant; how was I supposed to volunteer while I was working, especially when the two felt so distant from one another? But once I felt the momentous energy of what it was like to join a conference call with Organizers from all over the country, I was hooked.

~ Aly Nagel"

"I am indefinable. I don't fit into any particular category."
— *Rufus Wainwright*

Women's March Los Angeles Timeline from Election night 2016 to Jan. 21, 2017

Nov. 8	Election Night
Nov. 9	Apply Permits, Plan a March
Nov. 10	Connected with DC March Organizers
Nov. 12	Connect with other LA Organizers Online
Nov. 14	Permit Accepted for Review LAPD
Nov. 16	Map on Proposed Route
Nov. 22	Organize with other Marches Planned in LA to join us/ Numbers
Nov. 23	Website Buildout
Nov. 28	We Get Approved 501-C3 Status
Nov. 29	Outreach Begins for Partners
Dec. 1	Connected with all CA Marchers (19)
Dec. 3	Website Launch
Dec. 4	Meeting with Westside Organizers
Dec. 7	Insurance Approved
Dec. 7	Readjust Route Map
Dec. 7	Merchandise Launched
Dec. 8	Meeting with Echo Park, Silver Lake, DTLA Organizers to get Boots on the Ground
Dec. 10	Meeting with Bakersfield, Rialto, Inland Empire for Organizers to Join Us
Dec. 12	Meeting with South LA, Compton, Watts and Rancho Dominguez Organizers
Dec. 12	First Women's March Collaboration Call/ Nationwide
Dec. 13	National Team Shares Logo
Dec. 15	Feminist Majority Joins Us
Dec. 15	ACLU Joins Us
Dec. 16	Women Veterans Join Us
Dec. 17	Santa Barbara Confirms 25 Buses
Dec. 17	19 Outreach for Speakers, City Officials Begins
Dec. 19	Request City for 3 More Blocks/ Olive, Hill, Broadway, Spring Streets
Dec. 19	We Have Nailed 100 Partnership Agrees
Dec. 20	Inform City, City of Hill, of Event Growth
Dec. 20	Bakersfield Confirms 5 Buses
Dec. 21	Meeting with 125 People Ambassadors Volunteers Training
Dec. 21	Metro & Dash Confirm Extra Passenger Trains
Dec. 21	1st Press Release Goes Out for LA March
Dec. 27	Confirmation of 9, Few Political Speakers
Dec. 27	Millenial Art Poster Making Launch
Dec. 28	Palm Desert 5 Buses
Dec. 30	22K Requested
Dec. 30	LAPD Invitation to Discuss Event @ Sight Safety
Jan. 2	UCLA Confirms 5 Buses
Jan. 3	Volunteers assist with answering phone calls and inquiries
Jan. 4	Street closures expand to close down an additional 3 roads
Jan. 5	LAPD, LAFD, DOT Meeting with City Officials for Safety, onsite first aid trainings take place
Jan. 6-25	Rally buses confirmed to arrive the morning of the March
Jan. 7	Security guard increase due to expected attendance rising exponentially
Jan. 8	Peace Ambassador training
Jan. 9	Additional street closure increases
Jan. 12	March start location moves to the corner of 5th & Hill
Jan. 18	Special event permit granted for attendance up to 500,000
	ASL interpreters secured
Jan. 19	City wide Department of Transportation alert for Women's March Los Angeles
	Final Speakers List for all stages confirmed
Jan. 20	Hilda Solis confirmed to be first speaker at Main Stage
	Setup for March begins on a rainy Friday, goes late into the night
Jan. 21	Women's March Los Angeles takes place, standing 750,000 strong, creating history in downtown Los Angeles

Women's March Los Angeles Special Thanks to:

It is with profound thanks and sincere appreciation to all those organizations and individuals who joined us for the historic Women's March Los Angeles on January 21, 2017.

Los Angeles Public Library
Center for the Pacific Asian Family
National Council of Jewish Women Los Angeles
Girls on the Run of Los Angeles
Global Women's Empowerment Network
Million Mamas
S.A.R.A.H
Alliance of Women Filmmakers
California National Party
360 Karma Women
Sand Sisters Los Angeles Inc.
Coalition to Preserve LA
Democratic Socialists of America - Los Angeles
New Directions for Women
East Los Angeles Women's Center
Project Caged Birds, Inc.
California NOW
Crossroads School for Arts & Sciences
South Bay United Teachers
Westside Center for Independent Living (WCIL)
Women Like Us Foundation
Haven Neighborhood Services
California Clean Money Campaign
Yes California
WriteGirl
Feminist Majority
New York Life Insurance Company
Future Vision Project
Standing Rock Women
Trinity Youth Services
Childrens Foundation of America
Allred, Moroko & Goldberg
Peace Over Violence
Planned Parenthood
Stand - LA
REALgirl Foundation Inc
Feminist Library On Wheels
ASSE International Student Exchange Programs
Shambahala Meditation Center of Los Angeles, Inc
Debt One Consultants
Los Angeles LGBT Center
NRDC
Lambda Legal
Multiracial Americans of Southern California (MASC)
NextGen Climate
Sierra Club Los Angeles Chapter
Women's Intercultural Network - Iranian Circal
SONA (Songwriters of North America)
Bray Ali for City Council 2017
Together We Will - Los Angeles
White People for Black Lives/ SURJJ/Aware LA
Las Fotos Project
California Council on Gerontology & Geriatrics
New York Life Insurance Company
Women Against Gun Violence
PopChips
Warbler Coffee Roasting
Girl Develop It - Los Angeles
The Keep A Breast Foundation
Rights Universal
Keys to Recovery
League of Women Voters of Los Angeles
If I Need Help
Iranian Progressives in Translation
SAHARA South Asian Helpline & Referral Agency
Take the Oath
Danny Trejo's Taco Truck
Indiana Jones "Chow Truck"
Rice Ball of Fire
Amazebowls
Sage Vegan Bistro
Boba ni Taco
Tasty Truck
Blast Ice Cream
Tropic Truck
Okamoto Kitchen
A Surfer Taco
Tender Grill
Atomic Cafe

PHOTO CREDITS

Abend, Joan 46

Acuña, Gina 44, 138

Aitkens, Irene 10, 18, 43, 160, 183

Alvarado, Karen 22

Baer, Daniel Rizik 78

Bauer, Susan 98

Bergen, Molly 185, 186

Bradshaw, Sarah 130, 138

Briggs, Terry 84

Brown, Rene Wang 86

Carrillo, Yelba 117, 121

Crafts, Ellen 8, 16, 199

Davidson, Chris 28, 31, 78

De la Sancha, Sylvia 46

Dee, Lisa 148

Elena, Alessandro 30, 70, 80, 81, 107, 109, 192,

Elliot 187, 188, 189

Ellis, Sarah Kate 92, 94, 95

Erikson, John 50

Fernandez, Sheila 130, 138

Flores, Claudia 34

Gengenbacher, Maria 168

Helmes, Yvonne 126

Hong-My Basrai 174

Huang, Rita Crayon 68

Hunt, Jamie 131

Jodat, Hanieh 20

Katz, Jerry 150

Klein, Ellen 38

Ladnier, Kavi 82, 117,

Laemmle, Nancy 136

Leher, Emily 152, 154

Lesak, Kim 56

Love, Liz 58

Maciosek, Chris 9, 26, 27, 30, 55, 126, 142, 143, 151, 162, 163, 164, 165, 166, 167, 172, 177, 179,

Mangel, Kathi 110

Manheim, Camryn 48

Martinez, Ricio 108

Miller-Wakeham, Brady 15, 64,

Nagel, Aly 196

Nasal, Elizabeth 145, 146

Navarro, Beth 194

O'Toole, Leeann 198

Pabon, Sylvia 100

Pacheco, Cristina 24

Pascal, David 71, 72, 73, 74, 91, 112, 113, 114, 115, 116, 144, 180, 181, 200

Pleune, Denise 139, 140, 182,

Puentes, Paula 75, 76

Rasmussen, Stephanie 134

Samson, Tracy 88

Santos, Judy 198

Stephenson, Heather 147

Tracy, Elizabeth 36

Wainwright, Rufus 198

Ward, Jennifer 184

Wolford, Eric 118

Yamamoto, Mia 66

Ziel, Carolyn 130